Quotable

WOODY

Quotable

WOODY

THE WIT, WILL, AND WISDOM OF WOODY HAYES, COLLEGE FOOTBALL'S MOST FIERY CHAMPIONSHIP COACH

MONTE CARPENTER

TowleHouse Publishing
Nashville, Tennessee

TowleHouse books are distributed by National Book Network (NBN),
4720 Boston Way, Lanham, Maryland 20706.

Library of Congress Cataloging-in-Publication Data

Hayes, Woody, 1913-1987.
  Quotable Woody : the wit, will, and wisdom of Woody Hayes, college football's
most fiery championship coach / [compiled by] Monte Carpenter.
        p. cm. -- (Potent quotables)
Includes bibliographical references.
  ISBN 1-931249-14-8 (alk. paper)
  1. Hayes, Woody, 1913-1987--Quotations. 2. Football coaches--United States--
Quotations. 3. Football--Coaching--Quotations, maxims, etc. I. Towle, Mike.
II. Title. III. Series.
  GV939.H35 A3 2002
  796.332'092--dc21

                                                                    2002002419

Cover design by Gore Studio, Inc.
Page design by Mike Towle
Inside photos provided by Ohio State University Photo Archives

Printed in the United States of America
1 2 3 4 5 6 — 06 05 04 03 02

CONTENTS

ACKNOWLEDGMENTS

THE BETTER PART of a week spent in Columbus, Ohio, researching this book was made all the more efficient and fruitful thanks to the help offered by the following people and institutions:

Bertha L. Ihnat, manuscripts assistant, Ohio State University Archives;

Julie A. Petersen, audiovisual curator, Ohio State University Photo Archives;

the Columbus Public Library and its staff;

and Steve Snapp, Ohio State University assistant athletics director.

Jim Otis and Lou Holtz provided support and encouragement for this project. Thanks, guys.

I thank my wife Holley and son Andrew for giving me the slack to be gone for days or sequestered for hours at a time pulling this book together. They have done this time and time again with numerous books, and I am forever grateful.

I thank God and His son Jesus Christ for always watching over my family, me, and my work.

If you're going to fight in the North Atlantic,
you've got to train in the North Atlantic.
—Woody Hayes, addressing players who
griped about having to practice in bad weather

INTRODUCTION

WOODROW "WOODY" HAYES was a Big Ten Conference icon for nearly three decades as the gruff, tough football coach for the Ohio State University Buckeyes. From 1951 through 1978, Hayes patrolled the sidelines at Ohio State, often ranting and raving, all the while pushing his Buckeye squads to among the elite of college football's finest and most-respected programs. His teams won three national championships, came close to winning a half-dozen more, and won more than two hundred games during a twenty-eight-year span that included some of the most colorful and confrontational moments in collegiate sports history. Given to occasional outbursts that saw him break yard markers in two, berate officials, and even punch an opposing player in a fit of frustration, Hayes also was a very successful motivator of men and molder of character.

Hayes was a throwback to another era, when football coaches were accepted as, and even expected to be, the civilian equivalent of military commanders, exhorting their troops and pushing the players to the limits of their capabilities. In fact, Hayes was a serious student of military history, an avowed admirer of General George Patton and a walking encyclopedia of famous battles of bygone decades and centuries.

Hayes didn't have a soft spot for much of anything and he was not afraid to dress down players in front of others for the sake of correction. And he *hated* to lose. Couldn't stand it. Yet he also expertly understood the game's intricacies and was second to none when it came to teaching his players and assistant coaches the finer points of football. Although Hayes ruled with an iron fist—some would even call it fear—he earned the respect and loyalty of players because Hayes played fair. He insisted on good sportsmanship, and would hear a player or assistant coach out if that player or coach had a legitimate grievance to bring before him. It's no wonder that Hayes compiled a sparking 205-61-10 record at

Ohio State that included thirteen Big Ten championships in addition to the three national titles.

Even though Hayes was one of college football's most recognized and winningest coaches, he also was one of the lowest paid in his profession—by choice. He alienated many with a temperament prone to anger and blunt words—occasionally profane—that cut no slack and were a world apart from political correctness. Fallacies and all, he had admirers numbering in the millions and ranging from U.S. presidents to middle-class moms.

Away from the frenzy and intensity of the field, Hayes could be a delightful conversationalist on a variety of topics. His surprisingly soft voice and expert elocution befitted his strong educational background, and his words—many of which are expressed here in *Quotable Woody*—testify to his wit, will, and wisdom.

Quotable

WOODY

ACCESSIBILITY

1. If your number isn't listed, the people who want to unload their feelings on you will find the number from some other source. Then they'll bother you to death because they know they have the edge. But if you make yourself available and sort of roll with the punch, the cranks will get tired of it and stop bothering you.

    —explaining why he and Anne listed their home telephone number in the Columbus phone book

ALUMNI

2. You hear much talk about alumni firing coaches, and I don't believe it works that way at all. I think it's the players who fire the coaches, and the alumni are only going to come into the picture after this has happened.

ANNE

3. The perfect buffer. Not only does she understand me better than I understand myself, but she understands my job and the time it takes.

APATHY

4. Boys, I don't want you on the football field if you're going to show any signs of apathy. Apathy: Avoid it like the plague.

   —addressing some of his players during one of his morning classes on word power, this time giving a brief lesson on apathy

ATTITUDE

5. You don't live in the past.

6. You don't just laugh your way to victory.

   —explaining why he never picked comedies as the movie of choice to show players the night before a game

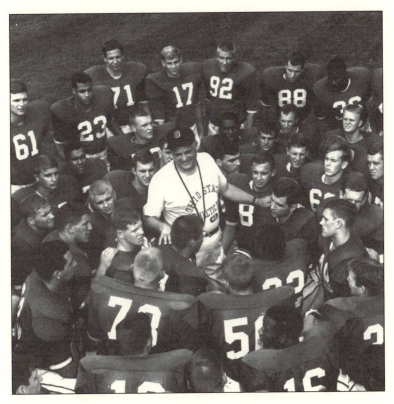

"Boys, I don't want you on the football field if you're going to show any signs of apathy."

BLOCKING

7. I believe that downfield blocking is 90 percent mental and 10 percent physical. The reason most blocks are missed is that the blocker takes his eye off the target, looking around to see if the play is going that far. That shows a lack of confidence by a blocker in his teammates—a confidence we'll work to instill.

CARS

8. I've noticed something about cars. Your real big cars and your real little cars are the ones that get stuck in the snow. Your medium-sized cars always keep moving along.

CHALLENGE

9. I probably muffed a lot of chances to be a nice guy. But there was no real dissension on the squad. Our kids always met the challenge. Perhaps they weren't too well coached, but they met the challenge.

—discussing his early days at Ohio State

CHARACTER

10. There's a lot of silly talk about building character in college football—and I happen to believe in it.

11. We concentrate on character. We talk to their parents, their teachers, their principals, coaches, ministers, and priests. If a kid doesn't have character, they don't have a chance.

    —*explaining his top priority when it came to recruiting*

12. The football player has got to be a better human being than the other students on campus. He's got to have cleaner habits. He's got to work harder. He's got to schedule classes earlier to have time for practice.

CHEATING

13. I don't want any damned cheaters around me. If a man will cheat, he'll break his word. The first thing I want is character.

14. Our whole show is based on wanting to win, and if you can do it cleanly, how can you top it?

15. Did I turn in (to the NCAA) the team (Michigan State) that cheated in our league? . . . You're damn right I did. And I'll do it again if necessary.

COACHING

16. The thing you have to do is go back each year and review what actually wins for you. You'll find it's the discipline on your squad and your morale and how you handle your players and how well you bring them along. Those are the things on which you win rather than all the technical ideas that all of us have.

17. All players simply don't learn at the same rate of speed or with the same degree of mastery. If we see a player making a mistake, we don't just get him out of there and run the play with somebody else just because the first kid doesn't learn very fast. That would be an indictment of our coaches. We just think we've got to spend extra time on the player.

18. Now take the football coach. What he's doing is giving a final examination, not just once a semester, but every week for at least ten weeks. His expertise as a teacher is on the line every Saturday. How well has he prepared his team for that final exam every game day? That scoreboard is going to tell you.

19. Good plans must always include time for individual coaching, for it is this area in which the greatest improvement is made.

20. For our first three years at Ohio State, I supervised more than I coached, and I managed to get into everyone's way.

COLLEGE PROFESSORS

21. What you say about me and about football may or may not be true. But I can tell you one thing that is very certainly true . . . I can do your job, but you can't do mine!

   —*to an OSU professor who had been critical of Hayes*

COMMERCIALIZATION

22. Football is in a state of flux; it's being overcommercialized. For years our games started at 1:30. Now they're starting at 12:30 and 3:30. Why? Television—so they can sell more Wheaties!

COMMUNICATION

23. Over the years I have gained excellent knowledge and great insight into the game by discussing it with my players, for quite often a player will come up with a suggestion or a thought that can certainly help.

24. An important factor in any good organization is communication. This means each man must not only hear, but the coaching expressions that are used must mean the same to each player and to each coach.

COMPUTERS

25. The computer can cause us a lot of trouble if we don't learn how to work it, because we'll have a lot of dummies on our hands. If we learn about computers, we're in the ballgame.

"Over the years I have gained excellent knowledge and great insight into the game by discussing it with my players."

CONVICTION

26. The Bible says turn the other cheek, but I'll be damned if I'll tell my kids to do that when they'll just get it fractured.

—explaining the time he ran sixty yards down the sideline to berate officials who he believed were letting the opposing defense get away with too much

CRITICS

27. The older I get, the less I care about what they say. I have to level with Woody Hayes; I don't have to level with them.

DEFENSE

28. The defense wins the upsets.

29. The goal-line defense is more an attitude than it is a precise set of techniques.

30. There are many thoughts that go into the building of a sound defense. Important among them is that we must always defend the open side first. Our pictures show that 84 percent of plays originate on or within four yards of a hash mark. This means that as the ball is snapped, there is twice as much area to the open side to defend as there is into the sideline.

31. Football is an equation. And the offense is given the advantage of the starting count and the knowledge of the attack area—the when and the where. On the other side of the equation, the defense is given the advantage of the use of hands and arms, and we must exploit this advantage to the fullest.

32. We've always taken great pride in taking away an opponent's best play and thereby reducing the efficiency of their best players. For many years we've had an expression: "Make them beat us left-handed."

33. A great pass defense is a combination of three factors—a relentless rush, intimidation of the receivers by bumping them and keeping them from getting into their pass patterns, and a sound zone coverage.

34. Hayes's Predetermined Goals for the Defense:

Give up seven points or less

Score or set up two scores inside the forty-yard line

No touchdown passes against us

Hold them to less than 250 yards total offense

No enemy play—pass or run—of more than twenty yards

Do not give up more than three consecutive first downs

Destroy 25 percent of their passes

Hold foe to 40 percent completion of passes per game

No penalties against us

We field all punts properly

We average at least ten yards on punt returns

We keep all kickoff returns inside their thirty-yard line

DIRTY PLAY

35. If there's dirty football played against my players, what do you think is going to happen? They're going to go right back the same way, and that's what happens between nations so many times; and reprisal is as vicious as it can be.

36. It's safe to say that no coach teaches dirty football. However, that isn't always enough. A coach has to lean over backward to prevent his youngsters from gaining the false impression that he would like to have them try anything.

DISCIPLINE

37. Football is discipline; discipline which starts with the coach but (which) must become the player's own discipline.

38. For us, discipline implies disciples, for the player will first believe in the coach as a person before he will accept fully the teachings of that coach.

DISCRETION

39. Be damned careful what you say. Not a one of them wants you to win. But I don't expect you to carry a chip on your shoulder like I do.

    —to his players one of the times before they played in the Rose Bowl

EDUCATION

40. Football is a $2 million business at Ohio State—which means that the twenty-two boys on the starting team bring in about $100,000 apiece in gate receipts each year. Think of that. And what do they get in return? . . . What they get is $1,300 a year in room, board, tuition, and books—the opportunity to get an education. And I'm going to see that they get that education. We certainly owe them that.

41. If we bring a young man to Ohio State University and don't do everything possible to see that he gets an education, we are cheating him.

42. I told my players they were coming here to get an education, otherwise I was knocking 'em out. Now they keep 'em eligible. When they get out of pro ball, they're damn bums because they don't know how to work. Do I sound bitter? I am.

43. They talk about grades now as if it was new. Hell, no. I was controlling grades thirty-five years ago. I didn't send them to study hall. I met them there.

44. They're talking now about all of this tutoring you need for athletes. We were doing that thirty-five years ago.

45. Do you know who the best history tutor on campus was? I was. Damn right.

46. I may never become very sophisticated, but the idea that education is important was literally hammered into me.

47. Athletes work harder for their A's, making them the best "A" students on campus. They spend three hours a day practicing and in the locker room before sitting down to study.

EMOTIONS

48. I probably have more trouble controlling my emotions now than I did when I was a young man in my fifties.

—speaking at age sixty-three

49. I just can't control my temper.

50. I've always been a high-strung individual. That's my artistic temperament coming loose.

ENTHUSIASM

51. I think the only way a man can maintain his enthusiasm for his job beyond a certain point is to be able to see his job in the larger context— the sublime context.

EXCELLENCE

52. The football coach should be a big enough man that he wants every sport and activity in that school to excel.

FAMILY

53. When I was growing up, our family gathered around the dining table right after church on Sunday and discussed anything and everything of interest. We wore our Sunday best, and Mother set the table with the best linen, best china, and candles. Sometimes our talks would last three hours.

54. I went to my dad's school for eleven years, and I believe there's nothing tougher than being the school superintendent's son.

> *—Woody's dad, Wayne B., was superintendent*
> *of schools in Newcomerstown, Ohio.*

FANS

55. Ninety percent of the coaches would be delighted with a 9-3 record. All they (fans) want you to do is win all the time. Fans are fickle.

> *—referring to circumstances surrounding Earle Bruce, his successor*
> *at Ohio State, who was never fully embraced by Buckeyes' faithful*
> *who saw the glass as half empty during six consecutive 9-3 seasons*

FOCUS

56. I try to get six or seven hours' sleep a night, and I try not to miss any meals. Just about all the time that's left goes on football.

FOOTBALL

57. I wish everything brought as much credit and as much teamwork and loyalty and just outright good honest fun to the university as football did.

58. This game used to be pretty important to me. It isn't anymore. Now it's just damn near everything. It represents and embodies everything that's great about this country, because the United States is built on winners, not losers or people who don't bother to play.

*—spoken two days before the 1978 Gator Bowl,
in what would turn out to be his last game*

59. We talked about what kind of football player Abraham Lincoln would have been, what position he'd have played. Defensive tackle, no doubt. He had those big, strong arms from chopping wood. His weakness: He was too tall; he'd have been double-teamed.

60. Football players are among the most gentle people in the world. Actually, the fellow you want to watch is that killer instinct—the guy who has something to prove. He may be a little fellow; he may have a chip on his shoulder; he may be a cripple; and he's going to show that he can measure up and he's going to do it by cutting the corners. A football player doesn't have to do that.

FORWARD PASS

61. I used to say three things can happen on a forward pass, two of them bad. I don't say that anymore, because I found out four things can happen on a forward pass. The fourth thing is, you can get fired.

FRESHMAN ELIGIBILITY

62. Freshmen may revolutionize college football. They can give your squad a vitality and enthusiasm it might not (otherwise) have. Everybody is going to have those few who can play, the exceptional kids. Take Archie (Griffin). All you have to do is hand him the ball.

FRIENDS

63. When you're winning, you don't need friends, and when you're losing you don't have 'em anyhow.

GENEROSITY

64. You can't pay back, but you can pay forward.

65. Emerson said that the more you give, the more you get in return. I was charmed by the fancy of this endless compensation. And doggone if it isn't true. It became the cornerstone of my coaching philosophy.

> —*speaking as a guest lecturer at Harvard in 1982 on the one hundredth anniversary of Ralph Waldo Emerson's death*

GOALS

66. Don't settle for low success.

HATE

67. I don't hate anybody. Hating will destroy you.

HERITAGE

68. Greene countians claimed I was born in Clark County, and Clark countians claimed I was born in Green County.

> —*referring to the fact that the Clifton, Ohio, house in which he was born straddled two county lines*

HEROES

69. You're doggone right I'm an idealist. I've been looking up all my life. I've been a hero worshipper from way back in the 1920s . . . I know of no one who isn't more beautiful when they're looking up.

70. A civilization without heroes isn't going to be a civilization much longer.

71. Without winners there can be no civilization, and without heroes there can be no winning. I can see a conscious or subconscious effort in our country to tear down heroes, and yet I ask: What achievement could there have been without heroes?

HISTORY

72. Then the Greeks got busy. And you know what they did? They went over and rebuilt their city and decided they needed a new type of government. They even had a name for it. *De-mo-cra-tos*. Did you ever hear of *de-mo-cra-tos*? People rule. People rule. That was the beginning of democracy.

    —Hayes giving a brief history lesson about the Greeks after they had defeated the Persians in war

HONESTY

73. I started the interview with an old navy expression: "Don't blow smoke." The only way to start such a meeting is with the truth.

    —on what he expected of his players when starting a meeting to discuss a disciplinary problem

74. An honest guy doesn't have a chance with a thief, because the honest guy is expecting the truth, and the liar or the thief is never going to give it to him.

    —as related by former player Kurt Shumacher

75. There are three kinds of liars. There are white liars, black liars, and there are statistical liars.

IMPROVEMENT

76. The greatest improvement in football has been not in the plays themselves, but in coaching the plays. And how a boy is taught is far more important than what he is taught.

THE INCIDENT

77. Of course I regret it. Who got hurt the most by it?

> —*referring to his punching a Clemson player in anger during the 1978 Gator Bowl, an act which resulted in his dismissal*

INJURIES

78. You don't get hurt when you run straight ahead.

79. We're so far ahead of other schools in the matter of protecting our players that it's pitiful.

    —*explaining why he had his players consistently do neck exercises, take an annual electroence phalogram of their heads for comparison later should they suffer a head injury, and change uniforms halfway through a game or practice on a hot day to avoid heat injury*

INTEGRITY

80. What kind of country would have drug smugglers at the head of it?

    —*referring to Panama during canal treaty negotiations*

INTENSITY

81. Listen, I'm not mellow. I'm the same guy I've always been, and I'll tell you this, the minute I think I'm getting mellow, then I'm retiring. Who ever heard of a mellow winner!?

JOB SECURITY

82. I didn't come here for the security; I came here for the opportunity.

83. I hold a job because I win. I wouldn't want to hold a job because of the number of friends I might have.

JUVENILE DELINQUENTS

84. I'm often asked to talk to juvenile delinquents, but I refuse. I don't know anything about juvenile delinquents. The boys I get are quality.

LANGUAGE

85. I don't want to sound pedantic, but the English language is a great language—fluid; it comes from many sources, and it's certainly not static.

LEADERSHIP

86. I'm not a law-and-order man. I'm a law-and-orderly man. . . . We control by attitudes rather than rules.

87. Never make a decision to placate a subordinate.

LIFE

88. The only way we got beaten was if we got a little fatheaded, if we didn't train well, if we had dissension on the squad, if we didn't recognize our purpose in life.

89. I'd have to be greedy or stupid or both if I didn't appreciate the fact that I've had just about the best life a man could ever have.

LOYALTY

90. Loyalty is a two-way street, not a blind alley.

91. Often nowadays, when a new head coach takes over, he fires every coach who is there. He does so on the excuse that he must have full loyalty. I feel that where there are good men, I can always get loyalty.

MANAGEMENT

92. We have no assistant coaches. Our coaches assist no one—they coach. Each coach is assigned duties that are commensurate with his abilities.

MEDIA

93. Tell the truth or say nothing. To mislead the press is neither ethical nor sensible.

94. You get doggone tired of cameras being pushed in your face. I'm fed up with it. I make no apologies.

95. A coach and his squad are entitled to some privacy.

    —explaining why he forcibly removed two reporters from the locker room after a 17-0 loss to Southern Cal in 1959

96. We once beat Wisconsin on information that we read in the student newspaper. The student writer had talked with a Badger player and reported changes made during practice that week. It clued us to the fact that Coach (Milt) Bruhn was changing to a split-T for our game. . . . That's a damn good reason to keep players from talking to reporters.

MICHIGAN

97. You're going to Michigan? Why, you dumb, no-good (bleep bleep)! You go right ahead! You go there and when you play against Ohio State we'll just see whether you gain a yard against us all day. We'll break you in two.

    —according to an unnamed assistant coach, this is what Hayes said to a prized fullback during a phone conversation in which the recruit told Hayes he was picking Michigan over Ohio State

"It's amazing how many fair-weather friends you discover when you lose two straight."

98. I said, Keep going! I don't spend five lousy cents in the state of Michigan. We'll make it to the Ohio line if we have to get out and push!
    —*regarding a recruiting trip to Michigan with assistant coach Ed Ferkamy with the gas-gauge needle pointing toward E*

99. From the very beginning, I knew the meaning of the Michigan game, even though I never appreciated the intensity until I was involved in it.

100. It's amazing how many fair-weather friends you discover when you lose two straight.
    —*after losing to Michigan, for a second straight year, in 1971*

MISTAKES

101. Mistakes are the greatest enemies of consistent football. Penalties, fumbles, interceptions, missed assignments, and poorly called plays can do more to stop our attack than anything our opponents can do.

102. Eliminate mistakes in football and you'll never lose a game.

103. No back in history ever has been worth two fumbles a game.

MONEY

104. I've never worried about money because I'm afraid that money would spoil me.

MORALS

105. Those people are trashy. I don't go for people like that. No, we don't need stuff like that.
—explaining why he wouldn't send Ohio State players picked for Playboy's Preseason All-American team to Chicago for a photo shoot

MOTIVATION

106. If you want to motivate a person, give him personal attention; secondly, show him improvement. When he sees that, he's going to stick with it.

107. I don't motivate players. I get them to motivate themselves.

108. We all have a tendency to be lazy . . . to ease off at times. That's why you need good teachers and good coaches to push you a little bit.

109. I'm cheating my players if I don't get the best out of them.

110. When people get emotional, they do great things. Yeah. And I wanted them mad so they'd do it. If they didn't, I'd kick them out. They're always better than they think they are.

111. We ask a player as he comes off the practice field and walks through the iron gate, to look up at the great stadium in which he will play and say to himself, "I am a better football player today than I was yesterday."

112. In football we always said, ". . . That other team can't beat us. We have to be sure that we don't beat ourselves." And that's what a person has to do, too—make sure they don't beat themselves.

113. You lose us a ballgame, and, by God, I'll throw you off the squad.

    —chewing out a player in practice who had missed the same assignment several times

RICHARD NIXON

114. That man is more astute in watching a football game than any man I've ever seen. You can't believe it. He'll ask, "Why did you do this? Why did you do that?" And you better have the answers.

OFFENSE

115. Our offensive football is based upon the principle that we must first establish a sound running attack. . . . A well-coached and well-manned running attack is the most consistent factor in football. We used the word "consistency" to denote the success of a play, for a "consistent" play is one which has gained at least three yards. If each play gains three yards, it is almost a mathematical certainty that at least one of the three plays will gain considerably more than three yards, so that possession of the ball is the net result.

OFFICIATING

116. I'm not telling you what to write, but all Big Ten games—except one—were very well officiated last Saturday. I won't say which one wasn't.

117. I respect the job the officials do, but just want to be sure they do it better.

OHIO STATE

118. Today is the greatest day of my life. I appreciate it so much to get to come here and talk to our graduating class at the Ohio State University, the great, great university.

    —from his commencement speech at Ohio State in 1986

119. I try to make something for Ohio State football that people can look up to, and, believe me, they do.

PERSEVERANCE

120. The great thing about football is that when you get knocked down, you get up and go again. You don't lie there and moan and groan and rail against the fates.

121. You look at so many of these men here and it's obvious why they were so successful. They got decked. They got their rears knocked off, but they got up.

     —speaking at a convention that included other sports legends such as baseball players Stan Musial and Satchel Paige, and heavyweight boxing champion Jack Sharkey

122. I was getting terribly, terribly tired. I should've quit about three years before I did. But I didn't have a coach ready for the job, and I didn't want to let my coaches down when I quit by having them out of jobs.

PITY

123. There is one luxury the coach cannot afford—it is the luxury of self-pity. When a coach resorts to this psychological mechanism, his days in the profession are numbered.

124. You cannot feel sorry for yourself because that's what leads to drugs, what leads to alcohol, to those things that tear you apart.

POP CULTURE

125. The kids went to see that *Easy Rider*, and they were so depressed by it they didn't play well.

       —explaining the Buckeyes' supposedly lackluster performance in a 43-7 victory over Minnesota in 1969, after showing his players a movie the night before

126. We talk all the time about role models, but with all the cheap trash on TV it's no wonder kids are befuddled and lose a sense of values. America is in need of heroes.

PRACTICE

127. You screwed us up just about enough for one
      day, haven't you?

      —to a player during a practice

PRAISE

128. Blame is safer than praise. And that's what I
      tell my boys all the time—that this niceness
      from people complimenting you can be what
      kills you. It can be deceiving.

PREPARATION

129. I believe in overlearning. That way you're sure.

130. Well, the hay's in the barn.

      —usual comment after a Friday practice before a game

"They can call me anything, just so they don't call me 'a nice old man.'"

PRIDE

131. It's only a road, but it's a good road.

> —*remarking to a writer about the fact that a street in Columbus had been named after him*

132. They can call me anything, just so they don't call me "a nice old man."

PROGRESS

133. This nice lady came up to me and asked, "What was the score of your Illinois game?" and I said, "27-7." Then she asked, "What was the score of your Michigan game?" and I said, "27-7." She commented, "You aren't making much improvement, are you?"

> —*telling of a brief conversation he had with a Buckeye fan following back-to-back upset victories over Illinois and Michigan in 1952, his second season*

PSYCHOLOGY

134. In all my years here I've sent only two of my players to a psychiatrist, and in both cases the problems had nothing at all to do with football. One kid was an exhibitionist. The other kid got all caught up in religion.

QUARTERBACKS

135. To eliminate mistakes you have to pick the right quarterback. That's why I keep a superior passer on the bench and play a boy who is less spectacular but steady and sure. The five big mistakes in football are the fumble, the interception, the penalty, the badly called play, the blocked punt—and most of these originate with the quarterback. Find a mistake-proof quarterback and you have this game won.

RACE

136. The only problem I ever had with Negro football players at Ohio State was in 1959. We lost five ballgames that year because we didn't have enough of them. They're great athletes and they're great kids.

RECOGNITION

137. When you come out of that stadium an hour and a half after a game and there's no one out there to congratulate you, it gets pretty lonely. You love it when a little kid happens to come up and say, "Good game, Mr. Hayes."

RECRUITING

138. Now we think you're a 100-percenter, son. You come with us, dig in your heels, and prove you're the best. You just have to ask yourself whether you're man enough to be a Buckeye.

139. Naturally, we're going after the great ones at any position and in any numbers we can land them, but at Ohio State we don't try to overdo it.

140. I've found that the better person he is, the better his potential as a player regardless of his skill potential. So I look for that good home background and a good relationship between the boy and his family.

141. Some of our best recruiting is done by professors who don't know a lateral pass from a fullback draw, but they sure know how to answer a boy's questions.

142. That's easy. We go out and find good linemen.
    —*on why his program had a knack for churning out so many great running backs*

"Some of our best recruiting is done by professors who don't know a lateral pass from a fullback draw."

143. Dirty money leaves tracks!

144. I find good homes wherever I go. The amount of money in the home has very little to do with it.

REMINISCING

145. I hate to reminisce. That always softens people. You think about the good things and forget the bad.

RESILIENCE

146. Those Japanese got the hell kicked out of 'em—and nobody had it coming more. But they learned from that defeat and built themselves a great nation. They learned you've got to dust yourself off and go at it again.

147. Mental toughness, the ability to withstand pressure, to rise above hardship and disappointment, is a real test of man's leadership ability.

148. Kids are
      buoyant;
      they snap
      back.

RESPECT

149. Once a youngster learns self-esteem, he can pass it on to other people. You can't respect somebody else until you've learned to respect yourself.

150. I'd like to be respected for my integrity. And respected for the interest in the people I coached. And I try to be a good American citizen.

ROSE BOWL

151. I charted the Rose Bowl when I was a sophomore in high school and we got our first radio. I'd get a big cardboard, and I'd chart every play.

152. We had a secret agreement among ourselves
     that anyone who mentioned roses would get a
     punch in the nose—unless it was a lady over
     eighty.
     —response in 1955 to clamoring fans excited about the team's
     Rose Bowl hopes even with four games remaining on the schedule

153. I don't agree with those twenty-eight "no"
     votes, but I respect their integrity, if not their
     intelligence.
     —referring to when, in 1961, the Ohio State faculty council voted,
     28-25, to turn down a Rose Bowl bid, concerned that supposedly
     too much emphasis was being placed on football at the school

154. We have had to learn to accept defeat under
     pressure and that may help us now, although it
     is difficult to explain to the boys when, after
     fifteen years, the Rose Bowl is jerked out from
     under them.

155. There are five teams in the Big Ten I'd rate ahead of Southern Cal—Michigan, Iowa, Wisconsin, Minnesota, and us. I believe all are better all-around teams than the Trojans.

    —stirring up trouble after his Buckeyes had knocked off USC, 20-7, in the 1955 Rose Bowl

156. What was I supposed to do? Lie about it or tell them what I really felt?

RULES

157. I tell my players there are two things you don't do: no drugs and no haters. I won't tolerate either one on our squad.

158. Commissioner Wilson's decision comes as a terrible shock to all of us. All my life I have been taught to respect properly delegated authority, and for this reason I do not believe we should appeal the decision. This, however, does not mean that I agree with the severity of the penalty or the manner in which the investigation was made.

—responding to Big Ten commissioner
Kenneth L. Wilson's slapping Ohio State in 1956
with a one-year probation for illicit payments to players

SCHOOL SPIRIT

159. I am one of the coaches in favor of extending the halftime period to twenty minutes to give the band more time to perform. I know how much work the band does. They practice as much as we do.

SELF-EXPRESSION

160. Keeping it in is the way to get an ulcer.

SOCIETY

161. There is a segment of society which is not only against football but against anything that's well organized.

162. One of the chief problems we face in society now is that people question every decision. They don't accept anything without wanting to debate about it.

SPORTSMANSHIP

163. We use a bit of psychology when it appears bad feelings are developing between an Ohio State player and his opposition. We send word to the player to pick his man up after the next block or tackle. It's hard to play dirty with a guy who helps you up after a play.

Fastest 50 of 1963
W.W. Hayes
Michigan Stadium
11-30-65

"One of the chief problems in society now is that people question every decision. They don't accept anything without wanting to debate about it."

164. Our boys will show more in sportsmanship in one afternoon than any philosophy professor can teach all year.

SPRING PRACTICE

165. We're not here to laugh.

STEWARDSHIP

166. The most valuable gift you can give anyone is your time.

STRATEGY

167. The Persians got in the back door at Thermopylae, you know. A traitor showed them a new path through the mountains and they outflanked Leonidas.

> —*speaking extemporaneously at a Big Ten football press luncheon after another coach had casually mentioned Thermopylae*

168. Compared to
      the strategy of
      football, tactics
      on the field
      amount to
      almost nothing.
      A fleabite.

STUDENT PROTESTS

169. Football players never take part in demonstrations. The demonstration starters are little guys with briefcases who never get attention and have to prove their masculinity. Football players don't have to prove theirs.

SUCCESS

170. I've had good players. I think I'm a terribly lucky coach. Give me the same material as anybody else, I think I'll beat him, on luck if nothing else.

TEACHING

171. In teaching we must first realize that the most important factor is not how much the coach knows, but how much useful football knowledge the coach can impart to each player.

"Winning is the epitome of team effort, and we must keep that, and we must inculcate that into our football players." (Woody confers with quarterback Rex Kern.)

TEAMWORK

172. People complain that we are victims of a permissive society. Well, I'll tell you this—we don't have one player on my team who "does his own thing." We aren't permissive here. At Ohio State they do our thing.

173. Winning is the epitome of team effort, and we must keep that, and we must inculcate that into our football players.

174. Yes, yes, I would very much. So many of our liberals are against that word, but I am not. I think so many times we cheat a youngster when we don't tell him what we already know.

> *—responding to a reporter's follow-up question, regarding teamwork, if indoctrination is a good word he would use to describe what he does with his players*

175. Do you know where you get (strength)? You get it in the huddle. You get it by going back and getting a new play and running that same play together. That "together" is the thing that gives you the buildup to get ready to go again.

TOUGHNESS

176. Our kids are never brutal. Of course, that opposing quarterback better be careful about running a whole lot.

177. I've never seen a football player make a tackle with a smile on his face.

178. If you're good enough, you're big enough.

> —*to Howard "Hopalong" Cassady, who came to Ohio State claiming he weighed 175 pounds when he actually weighed 155. Cassady went on to win the Heisman Trophy.*

TRADITION

179. This is recognition. Not everybody can get his name in a headline, so when these kids know that their coaches have singled them out for outstanding performance, it means something. They know the fans notice those Buckeye leaves, too.

—on the school tradition of affixing Buckeye leaves to players' helmets

180. The mark of a great Buckeye is to rise to the occasion.

TRUST

181. I can't trust anybody back there! I go away for two weeks, and you kill me! I might as well kill myself right here!

—spoken while mountain climbing in the Alps, on vacation, upon learning that one of his running backs had flunked out of school

"This is recognition. Not everybody can get his name in a headline, so when these kids know that their coaches have singled them out for outstanding performance, it means something." (Hayes with Bob Hope)

WAR

182. Now the double-team block, of course, is the story of your First World War, very simple. Germany was caught in the double-team block, between the pressure from the Allies from the West—France and England—and then pressure from the Russians in the East. Now do you know what the Germans did to break the double-team block? They went to Switzerland and got a fella and sealed him up in a boxcar and sent him to Russia to foment a revolution just so they could break that double-team block . . . Of course, I'm talking about Lenin.

183. To me, football is a microcosmic reflection of the ideals, emotions, strategies, pitfalls, and problems of a society. Now go back to the battle of Salamis, where the Greeks beat the tail off the Persians. Now doesn't that take in so many of the things you see in a football game? Fear, determination, backs to the wall, homefield advantage— all those things you see in a football game. And that Battle of Salamis wasn't for the national championship, it was for the world championship.

184. A frontal attack is rarely considered good strategy in military warfare, but if well timed, a frontal attack can lead to victory.

185. You'd be surprised the things I learned from that man. He had great ideas on security, always had low casualty rates, and he was a no-nonsense guy.

    —*referring to General George Patton*

186. That war was not lost over there; it was lost here. . . . Those were good kids over there. They'd make a good football team.

    —*referring to the Vietnam War*

187. The men I talked to in Vietnam were in excellent spirits—I never heard a bit of complaining over there. The men had tremendous morale. . . . They're out there to get the job done, and if they don't it won't be because they're not trying.

    —*after returning from a 1967 trip to visit soldiers in Vietnam*

188. These wars always bring bigger problems than they settle. We can't have that. And yet it's up to us to have such a good democracy that those people want it, too.

WINNING AND LOSING

189. When we lose a football game and I look at myself in the mirror the next day, I feel like taking a punch at myself.

190. Maybe it's vanity; I just despise getting beat.

191. I'm so damned sick and tired of losing I don't know what to do!
    —after the Gator Bowl game in which he punched a Clemson player

192. Nobody despises to lose more than I do. That's what got me into trouble over the years, but it also made a man with mediocre ability into a pretty good coach.

193. This whole country has been built on one thing—winning.

194. We never apologize for winning, because that's exactly what we want to do.

195. You don't win games with alumni. You don't win games with friends. You win with players. You win with coaches.

196. I've hated to lose ever since I was a kid and threw away the mallets when I lost at croquet.

197. We expect to win. We play to win. I'll never come out moaning about how we don't have a chance, because I don't think it's fair to boys who have been doing their best for me.

WOODY ON WOODY

198. If people don't criticize Woody Hayes, there's something wrong with them. I walked by the mirror Sunday and almost took a swing at him.

199. That was as bad a game as I've ever coached. I was worse than the boys, and they were pretty terrible.

    —following a 7-7 tie with TCU in 1961

200. Not being at the top of the list gave me an advantage because I was not subject to the criticism and barbs that a frontrunner invariably experiences.

    —on his being hired in 1951 as a darkhorse candidate for the job

WORK ETHIC

201. Nothing in this world that comes easy is worth a dime.

202. It's when I hurry into something—that's when I don't do very well. That's why I'm a hermit, a recluse during football season. I have to work harder to do what comes easily to other people.

203. The only smarts I have are that I'm smart enough to know that I can outwork 'em.

204. If you give me a big enough head start, I can beat Jesse Owens.

205. Hard work never killed a person. It's the partying and socializing, late hours and the like, that affect so many people.

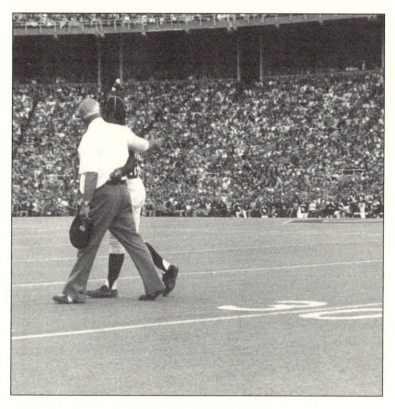

"Nothing in this world that comes easy is worth a dime."

OTHERS ON WOODY

STEVE HAYES

I STILL REMEMBER MY FATHER AS A MAN WHO
WAS GOING TO MAKE YOU GET THE BEST OUT OF
YOURSELF.[1]

BO SCHEMBECHLER

I LOVED WOODY HAYES . . . DAMMIT, IT'S A FACT
AND I'VE NEVER TRIED TO HIDE IT.[2]

CHARLIE BAUMAN

HE WAS SUCH A COMPETITIVE MAN. I DON'T
KNOW; IF I WAS IN HIS SHOES, MAYBE I WOULD
HAVE DONE THE SAME THING. IT DIDN'T HURT. I
DIDN'T EVEN FEEL IT.[3]

> —*Bauman was the Clemson middle guard
> who Hayes punched in the 1978 Gator Bowl*

DARYL SANDERS

WE SAT THERE FOR SEVEN HOURS WITHOUT A
GLASS OF WATER, WITHOUT ANYTHING. THE OLD
MAN TALKED, JUST SHARED HIS HEART. TALKED
ABOUT A LOT OF THINGS. IT GOT DARK OUT. IT
WAS DARK IN THE ROOM.[4]

> —*Daryl Sanders, a former OSU player,
> recalling when he and Archie Griffin
> visited Hayes at his home after the firing*

ESCO SARKKINEN

HE WAS A GOOD LISTENER AS LONG AS HE FELT
YOU WERE MAKING THINGS WORTHWHILE.[5]
—Sarkkinen was an assistant coach under Hayes

ANNE HAYES

FOOTBALL AND NINETY BOYS—THE FOOTBALL
SQUAD—CAME AHEAD OF ME, BUT I DIDN'T
MIND THAT. I SAID IT WAS BETTER THAN HAVING
ONE THIN BLONDE IN AN APARTMENT
SOMEWHERE.[6]

JIM PARKER

WOODY NEVER LUSTED FOR GOLD. HE WAS NOT
A GREEDY MAN.[7]

JOHN BOZIK

HE LIKED TO HAVE YOU CONSIDER HIM AN S.O.B., AND HE WAS DISAPPOINTED IF YOU DIDN'T.[8]

BO SCHEMBECHLER

PEOPLE DON'T RECOGNIZE THE SUBTLE NUANCES OF THOSE PLAYS THAT LOOKED SO SIMPLE. TAKE THE OFF-TACKLE PLAY. TRUTH OF THE MATTER IS, PROBABLY MORE THAN ANY OTHER COACH, HE REFINED EVERYTHING INCLUDED IN THAT PLAY TO MAKE IT SUCCESSFUL, NO MATTER WHAT YOU (THE DEFENSE) DID. THE LINE SPLITS HAD TO BE EXACT, AND THE BLOCKING SCHEMES JUST AS EXACT. THE BALL HANDLING LOOKED THE SAME, WHICH IS WHAT THE PUBLIC SEES. BUT THE INNOVATION WAS UP FRONT.[9]

LOU HOLTZ

WHEN I WAS AN ASSISTANT COACH AT OHIO
STATE (1968), IT BECAME OBVIOUS TO ME THAT
OUR ATHLETES WEREN'T THAT MUCH BETTER
THAN WHAT OTHER PEOPLE HAD, BUT THEY
THOUGHT THEY WERE SUPER.[10]

FRED PAGAC

TALK ABOUT LOVE AND HATE MOTIVATION; HE
HAD FEAR MOTIVATION.[11]
            —*Pagac played for Hayes in the early seventies*

ANNE HAYES

HE WOULDN'T HAVE LIKED ME IF I'D BEEN A
MILQUETOAST WOMAN. HE WANTED A
CHALLENGE. THAT WAS PART OF HIS NATURE,
AND I MADE UP MY MIND HE WAS GOING TO GET
IT FROM ME.[12]

LOU MCCULLOUGH

IF YOU HAD AN ARGUMENT WITH COACH HAYES, THE NEXT DAY IT WAS FORGOTTEN.[13]
        —*McCullough was an assistant coach under Hayes*

ARCHIE GRIFFIN

WOODY IS A GOD-FEARING MAN. IT'S NICE TO KNOW HE'S AFRAID OF SOMEBODY.[14]

RICHARD NIXON

I WANTED TO TALK ABOUT FOOTBALL. WOODY WANTED TO TALK ABOUT FOREIGN POLICY. YOU KNOW WOODY—WE TALKED ABOUT FOREIGN POLICY.[15]

                    —*Richard Nixon describing the*
            first time he met Hayes, which was in 1957

JOHN BRICKELS

WOODY WAS ALWAYS SUBJECT TO
TEMPERAMENTAL OUTBURSTS. MAYBE IT'S
BECAUSE HE WAS SMART, QUICK, AND A
PERFECTIONIST.[16]

*—Brickels was head coach at New Philadelphia
High School when Hayes was an assistant there*

ANNE HAYES

PEOPLE TALK ABOUT HOW DEVOTED WOODY IS
TO FOOTBALL. HE WAS JUST AS DEDICATED TO
THE NAVY. WHY, WE HAD BEEN MARRIED ONLY
FIVE DAYS WHEN HE ASKED FOR SEA DUTY.[17]

RIX YARD

WOODY STICKS TO WHAT HE BELIEVES IS RIGHT,
EVEN WHEN IT'S WRONG.[18]

—Yard was a Hayes assistant

HAROLD "CHAMP" HENSON

WOODY TOLD US BEFORE THE GAME THAT
THIS WOULD BE THE MOST IMPORTANT THING
WE'D EVER DO IN OUR LIVES. AND I AGREED
WITH HIM.[19]

> —*Henson, a fullback under Hayes,*
> *referring to Ohio State's 14-11 victory over*
> *Michigan in 1972 to clinch a Rose Bowl berth*

HUGH HINDMAN

THERE IS NOT A UNIVERSITY OR ATHLETIC
CONFERENCE IN THIS COUNTRY WHICH WOULD
PERMIT A COACH TO PHYSICALLY ASSAULT A
PLAYER. THERE WAS NO DIFFICULTY IN REACHING
THE DECISION.[20]

> —*Hindman, the athletic director at*
> *the time, referring to the 1978 Gator Bowl*
> *punch-throwing incident that led to Hayes's firing*

STEVE HAYES

HE DID WHAT HE SAID, MEANT WHAT HE SAID, AND YOU WATCH THAT LONG ENOUGH AND IT'S CONTAGIOUS. YOU'D ALWAYS GET A STRAIGHT ANSWER. SOMETIMES YOU WISH YOU HADN'T.[21]

UNNAMED ASSISTANT COACH

WITH WOODY, THERE'S NO QUESTION OF WHO IS IN SUPREME COMMAND. ESPECIALLY ON OFFENSE. YOUR DIRECTION AND COACHING TECHNIQUE IS UNDER THE GUN EVERY SECOND. IT'S HAIRY AT FIRST, BUT YOU LEARN TO LIVE WITH IT.[22]

DICK WALKER

Any assistant coach guilty of sending Hayes out on a recruiting trip for an overrated prospect knew there would be a price to pay when Hayes returned:

IT'S WORTH AT LEAST FIFTY MEGATONS. WASTING WOODY'S TIME JUST MIGHT BE THE WORST SIN OF ALL.[23]

—Walker was an assistant under Hayes

JOE PATERNO

Recruiting against Hayes was a brutal assignment:

UNTIL TEN YEARS AGO I HAD IT MADE. MY EXCURSIONS INTO THE NEW YORK CITY AND NEW JERSEY AREAS WERE LEISURELY AND LIMITED. SUDDENLY, I BEGAN TO RUN ACROSS WOODY HAYES EVERYWHERE I WENT. MY GOD, THERE WERE TIMES WHEN I'D BE GOING INTO A SCHOOL OR A BOY'S HOUSE AND THERE WOULD BE WOODY HAYES COMING OUT! NOW I'VE GOT TO MAKE THOSE EASTERN TRIPS EVERY WEEK OR SO, OR WOODY WILL MURDER US, BECAUSE YOU KNOW THE KIND OF IMPRESSION WOODY MAKES IN THE HOME.[24]

UNNAMED ASSISTANT COACH

MY GOD, I'M ON MY WAY TO BECOMING
ANOTHER WOODY HAYES![25]
—*the assistant speaking one year after leaving
Ohio State to take a head-coaching job elsewhere*

RICHARD NIXON

TWO THOUSAND YEARS AGO, THE POET
SOPHOCLES WROTE, "ONE MUST WAIT UNTIL THE
EVENING TO SEE HOW SPLENDID THE DAY HAS
BEEN." WE CAN ALL BE THANKFUL TODAY THAT
IN THE EVENING OF HIS LIFE, WOODY HAYES
COULD LOOK BACK AND SEE THAT THE DAY HAD
INDEED BEEN SPLENDID.[26]
—*Nixon eulogizing Hayes*

PAUL ZIMMERMAN

I'M ABLE TO SUSTAIN TWO VIEWS OF WOODY
HAYES. ONE IS OF WOODY AS A FOOTBALL
COACH, AND ONE AS A MAN WHOM I AS A
WRITER WOULD HAVE TO COVER ON MY JOB. I
KNOW HOW WOODY HAYES COACHES FOOTBALL,
AND IF I WERE A YOUNG PLAYER, I'D GIVE MY
LEFT TESTICLE TO PLAY FOR HIM. BUT I ALSO
KNOW HIS GENERAL OPINION OF THE PRESS, AND
AS A SPORTSWRITER, YOU COULDN'T PAY ME
ENOUGH TO COVER HIM ON A REGULAR BASIS.[27]
—Zimmerman is a longtime football writer

ANNE HAYES

I'D BE HARD PUT TO RECALL WHEN WOODY HAS
DONE ANYTHING MUCH AROUND THE HOUSE,
AND I DISCOVERED VERY EARLY IN THE GAME
THAT THAT'S THE WAY IT WAS GOING TO BE.[28]

LOU FISCHER

WOODY EXEMPLIFIES CONVICTION AND
DETERMINATION MORE THAN ANYONE I'VE EVER
MET. I'VE ALSO NEVER MET ANYONE WHO MAKES
SUCH A LASTING IMPRESSION ON YOU. IT'S
ALMOST PHYSICAL. GETS RIGHT INTO YOU.[29]
                    —*Fischer played at Ohio State under Hayes*

UNNAMED FORMER PLAYER

I RESENTED HIM RUNNING MY LIFE BY
CONFINING ME TO THAT DAMNED STUDY TABLE
FOR A WHOLE YEAR. I WAS TOO DUMB TO
REALIZE WOODY WAS DOING ME THE GREATEST
FAVOR OF MY LIFE.[30]

ANNE HAYES

I LIVE IN A MAN'S WORLD. ABOUT THE ONLY
GIRLS I KNOW ARE THE WIVES OF THE PLAYERS
AND THEIR GIRLS.[31]

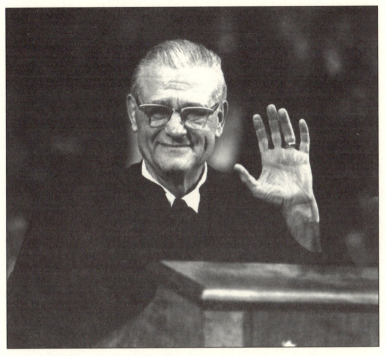

"I resented him running my life by confining me to that damned study table for a whole year. I was too dumb to realize Woody was doing me the greatest favor of my life." (Quote from an unnamed former player)

GERALD FORD

IT'S A GREAT HONOR TO BE HERE IN OHIO
TODAY—SOMETIMES KNOWN AS THE LAND OF
THE FREE AND THE HOME OF WOODY HAYES.[32]

—Gerald Ford, giving the
OSU commencement address in 1974

ANNE HAYES

OH, I NEVER CALL IT "THAT SCHOOL UP NORTH"
LIKE SOME PEOPLE. I CALL IT MICHIGAN,
STRAIGHT OUT. OF COURSE, WHEN I WRITE IT
OUT, I NEVER CAPITALIZE THE *M*.[33]

STEVE HAYES

HE NEVER CARED VERY MUCH ABOUT MONEY. I
THINK IF THEY HAD TOLD HIM IT WOULD COST
$20,000 A YEAR TO COACH AT OHIO STATE, HE'D
HAVE PAID IT. HE'S THE WORLD'S WORST
BUSINESSMAN.[34]

BUCKEYE FAN

THE DAY YOU DOTTED THE *i*, I NEVER CRIED SO
MUCH IN MY LIFE. OHIO IS NOT OHIO WITH YOU
GONE, COACH. AND FOOTBALL ISN'T FOOTBALL
EITHER.[35]

—a woman fan to Hayes after asking him to sign a
couple of photos of him sometime after his retirement

JACK FULLEN

IN WOODY HAYES WE HAVE A COACH WHO
COMMANDED HIS OWN SHIP IN THE PACIFIC;
WHO KNOWS WHAT IT IS TO BE BOMBED AND
STRAFED FOR KEEPS. HE'S GOT THE COURAGE TO
FACE THE COTTON PELLETS OF WORDS AND
INNUENDOES AND KEEP ON PLUGGING. AND
WHAT A PLUGGER.[36]

—Fullen was Ohio State's
alumni executive secretary at the time

ANNE HAYES

I FIGURE MY MISSION IN LIFE IS TO UNTENSE
WOODY. BUT DON'T GET THE IDEA THAT HE IS
PAST TENSE.[37]

JIM PARKER

WOODY COULD'VE SAVED HIS JOB IF HE HAD
COME OUT RIGHT AWAY AND APOLOGIZED, BUT
HE WAS SO BULLHEADED HE WOULD NEVER
APOLOGIZE FOR SOMETHING HE THOUGHT HE
WAS RIGHT ON.[38]

—referring to the 1978 Gator Bowl incident

TOM MATTE

I WAS A WORRIER. I WAS SO NERVOUS ABOUT
EVERYTHING, THAT WOODY GAVE ME ULCERS. I
WAS AFRAID OF WOODY, BUT HE DIDN'T KNOW
THAT.[39]

REX KERN

WOODY MEANT MORE TO US THAN JUST A
FOOTBALL COACH. IT'S HARD TO SAY JUST HOW
MUCH EFFECT HE HAD ON YOU. YOU DON'T
KNOW IF YOU HAD A LOT OF THESE QUALITIES
BEFORE YOU GOT HERE AND HE BROUGHT THEM
OUT. WOODY TAUGHT ME TO VALUE YOUR
EDUCATION, TO STAND UP AND FIGHT FOR
SOMETHING IF YOU BELIEVE IN IT.[40]

DARYL SANDERS

WOODY WAS ONE OF THE GREAT SALESMEN. HE
WAS VERY ENDEARING. . . . I'D NEVER BEEN
AROUND ANYONE WITH SUCH PASSION, ENERGY,
AND ARTICULATION.[41]

BOB VOGEL

IT BROKE MY HEART THAT HE WAS UNABLE, OR
UNWILLING, TO EVER RECEIVE JESUS, THAT HE
WAS NEVER ABLE TO LET THAT SHIELD DOWN
AND ALLOW PEOPLE TO LOVE HIM.[42]

   —*Vogel was another of Hayes's players at Ohio State*

ARCHIE GRIFFIN

I HAD HEARD ALL OF THE THINGS THAT YOU'D
HEAR IN THE PRESS ABOUT COACH HAYES—THAT
HE WAS TOUGH, THAT HE WOULD WORK YOU TO
DEATH. BUT THAT DIDN'T BOTHER ME, BECAUSE I
ALWAYS FELT THAT'S WHAT A COACH WAS
SUPPOSED TO DO.[43]

JIMMY CRUM

ON CAMPUS THERE WAS A GROUNDSWELL
REACTION, A MOVEMENT FOR BBB—BRING BACK
(PAUL) BROWN . . . SO WHEN WOODY GOT THE
JOB, IT WAS MET WITH MIXED EMOTIONS.[44]

> *—Jimmy Crum, a former Columbus*
> *TV sportscaster, remembering when*
> *Ohio State was searching for a new coach in 1951*

RONALD REAGAN

WOODY HAYES WAS A LEGEND IN COLLEGE
FOOTBALL. COLORFUL AND SOMETIMES EVEN
CONTROVERSIAL, HE CARED DEEPLY ABOUT HIS
PLAYERS, HIS TEAM, AND HIS SCHOOL.[45]

ANNE HAYES

DIVORCE, NO. MURDER, YES.[46]
—when asked if she had ever considered leaving Woody

JIM PARKER

WOODY COULD GET 120 PERCENT OUT OF AN
80 PERCENT GUY.[47]

TOM MATTE

IF YOU'RE WRONG, YOU DESERVE A KICK IN THE
ASS. YOU DON'T HAVE TO BEAT SOMEONE UP OR
ABUSE THEM, BUT YOU'LL LEARN . . . A LOT
QUICKER WITH DISCIPLINE. . . . I THINK THAT'S
WHAT WOODY DID, AND I APPRECIATE WHAT
WOODY DID FOR ME.[48]

RICHARD NIXON

I GOT TO KNOW THE MAN BEHIND THE MEDIA
MYTH, AND I FOUND THAT INSTEAD OF BEING
JUST THAT TYRANT YOU SOMETIMES SEE ON THE
FOOTBALL FIELD, THAT HE WAS ACTUALLY A
SOFTIE, A WARM-HEARTED MAN.[49]

TUG WILSON

COACH HAYES KNOWS FULL WELL THERE ARE
BETTER CHANNELS THAN PUBLIC DISCUSSION
FOR DISPOSING OF ANY QUESTIONS HE MAY WISH
TO RAISE REGARDING OFFICIATING OR PLAYER
CONDUCT. HE ALSO KNOWS FULL WELL THAT WE
DO NOT CONDONE DIRTY PLAY AS HAVING A
PLACE IN COLLEGE FOOTBALL. . . . HE HAS DONE
A DISSERVICE TO COLLEGE FOOTBALL BY HIS
BROAD CHARGES WHICH LEAVE THE PUBLIC
WITH AN IMPRESSION THAT COLLEGE FOOTBALL
IS DIRTY, FOR THIS IS NOT A FACT.[50]

—Wilson was a Big Ten commissioner
during part of Hayes's Ohio State tenure

SHIRLEY MACLAINE

WOODY IS LIKE A MAN WHO STRUTS LIKE A PEACOCK, CROWS LIKE A ROOSTER, AND WHEN HE GETS IN A BOWL, LAYS AN EGG. NO MATTER HOW MANY NASTY THINGS ARE SAID ABOUT YOU, WOODY . . . WHEN ALL IS SAID AND DONE, YOU CAN COUNT YOUR REAL ENEMIES ON THE FINGERS OF THE GIRL SCOUTS OF AMERICA.[51]

—speaking at a Woody Hayes roast

PAUL WARFIELD

HIS MISSION WAS NOT TO PRODUCE PLAYERS FOR THE NFL, BUT TO PRODUCE PLAYERS WHO COULD COMPETE IN SOCIETY.[52]

COLUMBUS RESTAURANT SIGN

IN ALL THE WORLD, THERE'S ONLY ONE WOODY.[53]

—sign outside the Jai Lai restaurant in Columbus, reportedly Woody's favorite local restaurant, following his death in March 1987

NOTES

1. Brondfield, Jerry, *Woody Hayes and the 100-Yard War*. New York: Random House, 1974, 260.
2. Hayes, Woody, *You Win with People!* 1973, 191.
3. *Ohio State University Monthly*, September 1973.
4. "Woody Hayes: The Football Coach." British Broadcasting Corp, 1978.
5. Ibid.
6. Ibid.
7. *Ohio State University Monthly*, April 1951.
8. *Washington Post*, sometime in 1984.
9. Weigel, J. Timothy, *The Buckeyes: Ohio State Football*. Chicago: Henry Regnery Co., 1974, 127.
10. Bynum, Mike, ed., *Woody Hayes: The Man and His Dynasty*. Gridiron Football Properties, 1991, 44, *Sports Illustrated*, September 24, 1962.
11. Ibid., 41, *Sports Illustrated*, September 24, 1962.
12. Ibid., 104, *Esquire*, October 1974.
13. Hornung, Paul, *Woody Hayes: A Reflection*. Champaign, IL: Sagamore Publishing, 1991, 134.
14. Brondfield, 276.
15. *Ohio State University Monthly*, September 1976.
16. Hornung, 150.
17. Brondfield, 117–118.
18. Ibid., 278.
19. *Hot Line to Victory*, 1969, 276.
20. Ibid., 284.
21. Brondfield, 26.
22. *USA Today*, September 14, 1984.
23. *You Win with People!*, 32.
24. Ibid., 136.
25. *Ohio State Lantern*, February 14, 1985.

26. Bynum, 40, *Sports Illustrated*, September 24, 1962.

27. "Woody Hayes: The Football Coach."

28. *You Win with People!*, 147.

29. Ibid., 148.

30. Ibid., 149.

31. Ibid., 150.

32. Ibid., 151.

33. Ibid., 154.

34. Brondfield, 133.

35. "Woody Hayes: The Football Coach."

36. *Ohio State University Monthly*, February 1952.

37. *Hot Line to Victory*, 3.

38. Ibid.

39. Hornung, 163.

40. Bynum, 43, *Sports Illustrated*, September 24, 1962.

41. Hornung, 75.

42. *USA Today*, September 14, 1984.

43. *Minneapolis Star-Tribune*, March 2, 1986.

44. Hayes's 1986 commencement address at Ohio State.

45. *USA Today*, September 14, 1984.

46. *Esquire*, August 1985.

47. *Ohio State University Monthly*, June 1964.

48. Natali, Alan, *Woody's Boys: 20 Famous Buckeyes Talk Amongst Themselves.* Wilmington, OH: Orange Frazer Press, 1995, 41.

49. *Columbus Dispatch*, March 13, 1987.

50. "Woody Hayes: The Football Coach."

51. Bynum, 108, *Esquire*, October 1974.

52. *Hot Line to Victory*, 282.

53. *The Booster*, August 20, 1986.

54. Levy, Bill, *Three Yards and a Cloud of Dust: The Ohio State Football Story.* Cleveland, OH: World Publishing Co., 1966, 262.

55. *Ohio State Lantern*, March 13, 1987.

56. Ohio State University Bureau of Public Relations, November 2, 1951.
57. "Woody Hayes: The Football Coach."
58. Natali, 46.
59. *USA Today*, September 14, 1984.
60. "Woody Hayes: The Football Coach."
61. Hornung, 4.
62. Bynum, 78, *Sports Illustrated*, October 9, 1972.
63. *Ohio State University Monthly*, October 1958.
64. Hornung, 90.
65. Ibid., 124.
66. *Ohio State University Monthly*, November 1962.
67. Hornung, 13.
68. Ibid., 5.
69. Ibid., 166.
70. Unknown source.
71. *Ohio State University Monthly*, September 1973.
72. Hayes's 1986 commencement address at Ohio State.
73. Hornung, 16.
74. Natali, 241.
75. *Ohio State Lantern*, August 19, 1985.
76. Bynum, 46, *Sports Illustrated*, September 24, 1962.
77. Hornung, 206.
78. Bynum, 47, *Sports Illustrated*, September 24, 1962.
79. Ibid.
80. *Ohio State Lantern*, August 19, 1985.
81. Bynum, 58–59, *Sports Illustrated*, November 11, 1968.
82. Brondfield, 72.
83. *Ohio State University Monthly*, September 1973.
84. *Ohio State University Monthly*, June 1964.
85. Hornung, 80.
86. Bynum, 68, *Life*, November 21, 1969.

87. *Hot Line to Victory*, 297.
88. Hayes's 1986 commencement address at Ohio State.
89. Hornung, 13.
90. Ibid., 22.
91. You Win with People!, 166.
92. Hayes, Woody, *Football at Ohio State*, 1957, 176.
93. Hornung, 166.
94. Bynum, 123, *New York Times*, December 31, 1978.
95. Levy, 360.
96. *Ohio State University Monthly*, September 1973.
97. Brondfield, 196.
98. *Reader's Digest*, September 1977.
99. *Dayton Journal Herald*, November 20, 1985.
100. Weigel, 204.
101. Levy, 330.
102. Ibid., 400.
103. Ibid.
104. "Woody Hayes: The Football Coach."
105. Ibid.
106. Hornung, 150.
107. Ibid.
108. "Woody Hayes: The Football Coach."
109. Ibid.
110. *Columbus Monthly*, May 1986.
111. *Football at Ohio State*, 179.
112. Hayes's 1986 commencement address at Ohio State.
113. "Woody Hayes: The Football Coach."
114. Hornung, 100.
115. *Football at Ohio State*, 1.
116. *Ohio State University Monthly*, November 1958.
117. *Ohio State University Monthly*, June 1969.

118. *Cleveland Plain Dealer*, March 13, 1987.
119. "Woody Hayes: The Football Coach."
120. Hornung, 221.
121. Bob Allen on Sports column, August 9, 1979, publication unknown.
122. *St. Petersburg Times*, November 22, 1986.
123. *Hot Line to Victory*, 279.
124. Bynum, *Sports Illustrated*, November 21, 1969.
125. *USA Today*, September 14, 1984.
126. "Woody Hayes: The Football Coach."
127. Bynum, 58, *Sports Illustrated*, November 11, 1968.
128. Ibid., 14, *Sports Illustrated*, October 24, 1955.
129. Hornung, 18.
130. *Washington Post*, sometime in 1984.
131. Weigel, 219.
132. Hornung, 24.
133. Bynum, 105, *Esquire*, October 1974.
134. Ibid., 45, *Sports Illustrated*, September 24, 1962.
135. Ibid., 42.
136. Natali, 43.
137. Bynum, 92, *Sports Illustrated*, September 9, 1974.
138. Brondfield, 171.
139. Ibid., 179.
140. Ibid., 188.
141. Ibid., 195.
142. "Woody Hayes: The Football Coach."
143. Levy, 380.
144. Hornung, 171.
145. *USA Today*, September 14, 1984.
146. *Hot Line to Victory*, 293.
147. "Woody Hayes: The Football Coach."
148. Ibid.

149. *Ohio State Lantern*, March 13, 1987.
150. Hornung, 10.
151. Bynum, 20–21, *Saturday Evening Post*, November 12, 1955.
152. Ibid., 34, *Sports Illustrated*, December 11, 1961.
153. Ibid.
154. Weigel, 145.
155. Ibid.
156. Hornung, 109.
157. Levy, 319–20.
158. *Ohio State University Monthly*, February 1955.
159. Bynum, 68, *Life*, November 21, 1969.
160. Hayes's 1986 commencement address at Ohio State.
161. Brondfield, 275.
162. Weigel, 232.
163. *Ohio State University Monthly*, February 1952.
164. *Ohio State University Monthly*, November 1962.
165. Bynum, 45, *Sports Illustrated*, September 24, 1962.
166. Hornung,224.
167. Ibid., 123.
168. Bynum, 46, *Sports Illustrated*, September 24, 1962.
169. *Ohio State University Monthly*, June 1964.
170. "Woody Hayes: The Football Coach."
171. *Hot Line to Victory*, 2.
172. Brondfield, 274.
173. "Woody Hayes: The Football Coach."
174. Ibid.
175. Hayes's 1986 commencement address at Ohio State.
176. Brondfield, 276.
177. *USA Today*, September 14, 1984.
178. Levy.
179. Brondfield, 112.

180. *Columbus Citizen-Journal*, November 23, 1985.
181. Brondfield.
182. Bynum, 106, *Esquire*, October 1974.
183. Ibid., 107.
184. Brondfield, 78.
185. *USA Today*, September 14, 1984.
186. *Columbus Dispatch*, March 29, 1985.
187. *Ohio State University Monthly*, September 1967.
188. Hayes's 1986 commencement address at Ohio State.
189. Hornung, 72.
190. Ibid.
191. Ibid., 198
192. Natali, 48.
193. *Time*, January 15, 1979.
194. Weigel, 233.
195. *Ohio State University Monthly*, September 1973.
196. Bynum, 8, *Sports Illustrated*, Oct. 24, 1955.
197. Ohio State University Bureau of Public Relations, November 2, 1951.
198. Weigel, 127.
199. Levy, 379.
200. *You Win with People!*, 38.
201. Hornung, 27.
202. Bynum, 67, *Life*, November 21, 1969.
203. Hornung, 27.
204. Ibid., 32.
205. *Ohio State University Monthly*, September 1973.

Others on Woody

1. Hornung, viii.
2. Ibid., x.
3. Ibid., xiii.
4. Natali, 125.
5. Hornung, 35.
6. Ibid., 51.
7. Ibid., 83.
8. Ibid., 118.
9. Ibid., 149.
10. Ibid., 150.
11. Ibid., 151.
12. Ibid., 52.
13. Ibid., 192.
14. Ibid., 232.
15. Ibid., 234.
16. Bynum, 12, *Sports Illustrated*, October 24, 1955.
17. Ibid., 27, *Saturday Evening Post*, November 12, 1955.
18. Ibid., 40, *Sports Illustrated*, September 24, 1962.
19. Ibid., 80–81, *Sports Illustrated*, December 4, 1972.
20. Ibid., 126, *New York Times*, January 1, 1979.
21. *Columbus Dispatch*, April 12, 1987.
22. Brondfield, 113.
23. Ibid., 177.
24. Ibid., 178–79
25. Ibid., 217.
26. Hornung, 235.
27. Brondfield, 241.
28. Ibid., 258–59.
29. Ibid., 267.
30. Ibid., 271.

31. *Ohio State Lantern*, December 6, 1962.
32. Unknown source, OSU Archives.
33. *The Sporting News*, November 20, 1978.
34. *Columbus Monthly*, September 1982.
35. *Washington Post*, sometime in 1984.
36. Levy, 282.
37. *The Sporting News*, November 20, 1978.
38. Natali, 74.
39. Ibid., 91.
40. Ibid., 175.
41. Ibid., 113.
42. Ibid., 110.
43. Ibid., 331.
44. Source not known.
45. *Columbus Dispatch*, March 13, 1987.
46. *Time*, January 15, 1979.
47. Natali.
48. Ibid., 102–3.
49. *Lorain Journal*, March 18, 1987.
50. *Ohio State University Monthly*, November 1958.
51. *Ohio State University Monthly*, March 1978.
52. *Ohio State Lantern*, March 13, 1987.
53. *New York Times*, March 18, 1987.

WOODY HAYES'S GAME-BY-GAME RECORD AT OHIO STATE

1951 (4-3-2)

Rank	Opponent (rank)	Site	Result	Score
#3	SMU	Home	Win	7-0
#7	Michigan State (#1)	Home	Loss	20-24
#9	Wisconsin	Away	Tie	6-6
#17	Indiana	Home	Loss	10-32
NR	Iowa	Home	Win	47-21
NR	Northwestern	Home	Win	3-0
#20	Pittsburgh	Away	Win	16-14
NR	Illinois (#3)	Home	Tie	0-0
NR	Michigan	Away	Loss	0-7

Final Rank: NR

1952 (6-3)

Rank	Opponent (rank)	Site	Result	Score
#20	Indiana	Home	Win	33-13
#15	Purdue	Home	Loss	14-21
NR	Wisconsin (#1)	Home	Win	23-14
#16	Washington State	Home	Win	35-7
#14	Iowa	Away	Loss	0-8
NR	Northwestern	Away	Win	24-21
NR	Pittsburgh	Home	Loss	14-21
NR	Illinois	Away	Win	27-7
NR	Michigan (#12)	Home	Win	27-7

Final Rank: 17th AP; 15th UPI

1953 (6-3)

Rank	Opponent (rank)	Site	Result	Score
#7	Indiana	Home	Win	36-12
#6	California	Away	Win	33-19
#3	Illinois	Home	Loss	20-41
#17	Pennsylvania	Away	Win	12-6
NR	Wisconsin	Away	Win	20-19
NR	Northwestern	Home	Win	27-13
#16	Michigan State (#5)	Home	Loss	13-28
NR	Purdue	Home	Win	21-6
NR	Michigan	Away	Loss	0-20

Final Rank: NR AP; 20th UPI

1954 (10-0, AP National Champions)

Rank	Opponent (rank)	Site	Result	Score
NR	Indiana	Home	Win	28-0
#14	California (#18)	Home	Win	21-13
#10	Illinois	Away	Win	40-7
#4	Iowa (#13)	Home	Win	20-14
#4	Wisconsin (#2)	Home	Win	31-14
#1	Northwestern	Away	Win	14-7
#2	Pittsburgh (#20)	Home	Win	26-0
#2	Purdue	Away	Win	28-6
#1	Michigan (#12)	Home	Win	21-7
#1	Southern Cal (#17)	Rose Bowl	Win	20-7

Final Rank: 1st AP; 2nd UPI

1955 (7-2)

Rank	Opponent (rank)	Site	Result	Score
#6	Nebraska	Home	Win	28-20
#8	Stanford	Away	Loss	0-6
NR	Illinois	Home	Win	27-12
#14	Duke (#11)	Home	Loss	14-20
NR	Wisconsin (#15)	Away	Win	26-16
#15	Northwestern	Home	Win	49-0
#11	Indiana	Home	Win	20-13
#10	Iowa (#20)	Home	Win	20-10
#9	Michigan (#6)	Away	Win	17-0

Final rank: 5th AP; 6th UPI

1956 (6-3)

Rank	Opponent (rank)	Site	Result	Score
#8	Nebraska	Home	Win	34-7
#4	Stanford	Home	Win	32-20
#5	Illinois	Away	Win	26-6
#5	Penn State	Home	Loss	6-7
#9	Wisconsin	Home	Win	21-0
#6	Northwestern	Away	Win	6-2
#7	Indiana	Home	Win	35-14
#6	Iowa(#7)	Away	Loss	0-6
#12	Michigan	Home	Loss	0-19

Final rank: 15th AP; NR UPI

1957 (9-1, UPI and Football Writers National Champions)

Rank	Opponent (rank)	Site	Result	Score
NR	Texas Christian	Home	Loss	14-18
NR	Washington	Away	Win	35-7
NR	Illinois	Home	Win	21-7
NR	Indiana	Home	Win	56-0
#12	Wisconsin	Away	Win	16-13
#8	Northwestern	Home	Win	47-6
#6	Purdue	Home	Win	20-7
#6	Iowa (#5)	Home	Win	17-13
#3	Michigan (#19)	Away	Win	31-14
#2	Oregon	Rose Bowl	Win	10-7

Final rank: 2nd AP; 1st UPI

1958 (6-1-2)

Rank	Opponent (rank)	Site	Result	Score
#1	SMU (#20)	Home	Win	23-20
#3	Washington	Home	Win	12-7
#5	Illinois	Away	Win	19-13
#3	Indiana	Home	Win	49-8
#2	Wisconsin (#13)	Home	Tie	7-7
#5	Northwestern (#11)	Away	Loss	0-21
#16	Purdue (#8)	Home	Tie	14-14
#16	Iowa (#2)	Away	Win	38-28
#11	Michigan	Home	Win	20-14

Final rank: 8th AP; 7th UPI

1959 (3-5-1)

Rank	Opponent (rank)	Site	Result	Score
#12	Duke	Home	Win	14-13
#14	Southern Cal (#11)	Away	Loss	0-17
NR	Illinois (#20)	Home	Loss	0-9
NR	Purdue (#6)	Home	Win	15-0
#20	Wisconsin (#12)	Away	Loss	3-12
NR	Michigan State	Home	Win	30-24
NR	Indiana	Home	Tie	0-0
NR	Iowa (#16)	Home	Loss	7-16
NR	Michigan	Away	Loss	14-23

Final rank: NR

1960 (7-2)

Rank	Opponent (rank)	Site	Result	Score
#20	SMU	Home	Win	24-0
#9	Southern Cal	Home	Win	20-0
#5	Illinois (#4)	Away	Win	34-7
#3	Purdue	Away	Loss	21-24
#9	Wisconsin (#11)	Home	Win	34-7
#8	Michigan State (#10)	Away	Win	21-10
#5	Indiana	Home	Win	36-7
#3	Iowa (#5)	Away	Loss	12-35
#10	Michigan	Home	Win	7-0

Final rank: 8th AP; 8th UPI

1961 (8-0-1, Football Writers National Champions)

Rank	Opponent (rank)	Site	Result	Score
#3	Texas Christian	Home	Tie	7-7
#8	UCLA	Home	Win	13-3
#7	Illinois	Home	Win	44-0
#7	Northwestern	Away	Win	10-0
#6	Wisconsin	Away	Win	30-21
#5	Iowa (#9)	Home	Win	29-13
#3	Indiana	Away	Win	16-7
#3	Oregon	Home	Win	22-12
#2	Michigan	Away	Win	50-20

Final rank: 2nd AP; 2nd UPI

1962 (6-3)

Rank	Opponent (rank)	Site	Result	Score
#2	North Carolina	Home	Win	41-7
#1	UCLA	Away	Loss	7-9
#10	Illinois	Away	Win	51-15
#6	Northwestern (#8)	Home	Loss	14-18
NR	Wisconsin (#5)	Home	Win	14-7
NR	Iowa	Away	Loss	14-28
NR	Indiana	Home	Win	10-7
NR	Oregon	Home	Win	26-7
NR	Michigan	Home	Win	28-0

Final rank: NR AP; 13th UPI

1963 (5-3-1)

Rank	Opponent (rank)	Site	Result	Score
NR	Texas A&M	Home	Win	17-0
NR	Indiana	Away	Win	21-0
#8	Illinois	Home	Tie	20-20
#4	Southern Cal	Away	Loss	3-32
NR	Wisconsin (#2)	Away	Win	13-10
#9	Iowa	Home	Win	7-3
#10	Penn State	Home	Loss	7-10
NR	Northwestern	Home	Loss	8-17
NR	Michigan	Away	Win	14-10

Final rank: NR

1964 (7-2)

Rank	Opponent (rank)	Site	Result	Score
#5	SMU	Home	Win	27-8
#5	Indiana	Home	Win	17-9
#4	Illinois (#2)	Away	Win	26-0
#2	Southern Cal	Home	Win	17-0
#1	Wisconsin	Home	Win	28-3
#1	Iowa	Away	Win	21-19
#2	Penn State	Home	Loss	0-27
#7	Northwestern	Home	Win	10-0
#7	Michigan (#6)	Home	Loss	0-10

Final rank: 9th AP; 9th UPI

1965 (7-2)

Rank	Opponent (rank)	Site	Result	Score
NR	North Carolina	Home	Loss	3-14
NR	Washington	Away	Win	23-21
NR	Illinois	Home	Win	28-14
NR	Michigan State (#4)	Away	Loss	7-32
NR	Wisconsin	Away	Win	20-10
NR	Minnesota	Home	Win	11-10
NR	Indiana	Home	Win	17-10
NR	Iowa	Home	Win	38-0
NR	Michigan	Away	Win	9-7

Final rank: NR AP; 11th UPI

1966 (4-5)

Rank	Opponent (rank)	Site	Result	Score
NR	Texas Christian	Home	Win	14-7
NR	Washington	Home	Loss	22-38
NR	Illinois	Away	Loss	9-10
NR	Michigan State (#1)	Home	Loss	8-11
NR	Wisconsin	Home	Win	24-13
NR	Minnesota	Away	Loss	7-17
NR	Indiana	Home	Win	7-0
NR	Iowa	Away	Win	14-10
NR	Michigan	Home	Loss	3-17

Final rank: NR

1967 (6-3)

Rank	Opponent (rank)	Site	Result	Score
NR	Arizona	Home	Loss	7-14
NR	Oregon	Away	Win	30-0
NR	Purdue (#2)	Home	Loss	6-41
NR	Northwestern	Away	Win	6-2
NR	Illinois	Home	Loss	13-17
NR	Michigan State	Away	Win	21-7
NR	Wisconsin	Home	Win	17-15
NR	Iowa	Home	Win	21-10
NR	Michigan	Away	Win	24-14

Final rank: NR

1968 (10-0, Consensus National Champions)

Rank	Opponent (rank)	Site	Result	Score
#11	SMU	Home	Win	35-14
#6	Oregon	Home	Win	21-6
#4	Purdue (#1)	Home	Win	13-0
#2	Northwestern	Home	Win	45-21
#2	Illinois	Away	Win	31-24
#2	Michigan State (#16)	Home	Win	25-20
#2	Wisconsin	Away	Win	43-8
#2	Iowa	Away	Win	33-27
#2	Michigan (#4)	Home	Win	50-14
#1	Southern Cal	Rose Bowl	Win	27-16

Final rank: 1st AP; 1st UPI

1969 (8-1)

Rank	Opponent (rank)	Site	Result	Score
#1	Texas Christian	Home	Win	62-0
#1	Washington	Away	Win	41-14
#1	Michigan State (#19)	Home	Win	54-21
#1	Minnesota	Away	Win	34-7
#1	Illinois	Home	Win	41-0
#1	Northwestern	Away	Win	35-6
#1	Wisconsin	Home	Win	62-7
#1	Purdue (#10)	Home	Win	42-14
#1	Michigan (#12)	Away	Loss	12-24

Final rank: 4th AP; 5th UPI

1970 (9-1, NFF National Champions)

Rank	Opponent (rank)	Site	Result	Score
#1	Texas A&M	Home	Win	56-13
#1	Duke	Home	Win	34-10
#1	Michigan State	Away	Win	29-0
#1	Minnesota	Home	Win	28-8
#1	Illinois	Away	Win	48-29
#2	Northwestern (#20)	Home	Win	24-10
#3	Wisconsin	Away	Win	24-7
#3	Purdue	Away	Win	10-7
#5	Michigan (#4)	Home	Win	20-9
#2	Stanford (#12)	Rose Bowl	Loss	17-27

Final rank: 5th AP; 2nd UPI

1971 (6-4)

Rank	Opponent (rank)	Site	Result	Score
#11	Iowa	Home	Win	52-21
#6	Colorado (#10)	Home	Loss	14-20
#14	California	Home	Win	35-3
#15	Illinois	Away	Win	24-10
#13	Indiana	Away	Win	27-7
#12	Wisconsin	Home	Win	31-6
#10	Minnesota	Away	Win	14-12
#9	Michigan State	Home	Loss	10-17
#16	Northwestern	Home	Loss	10-14
NR	Michigan (#3)	Away	Loss	7-10

Final rank: NR

1972 (9-2)

Rank	Opponent (rank)	Site	Result	Score
#3	Iowa	Home	Win	21-0
#5	North Carolina	Home	Win	29-14
#3	California	Away	Win	35-18
#4	Illinois	Home	Win	26-7
#4t	Indiana	Home	Win	44-7
#4	Wisconsin	Away	Win	28-20
#5	Minnesota	Home	Win	27-19
#5	Michigan State	Away	Loss	12-19
#9	Northwestern	Away	Win	27-14
#9	Michigan (#3)	Home	Win	14-11
#3	Southern Cal (#1)	Rose Bowl	Loss	17-42

Final rank: 9th AP; 3rd UPI

1973 (10-0-1)

Rank	Opponent (rank)	Site	Result	Score
#3	Minnesota	Home	Win	56-7
#3	Texas Christian	Home	Win	37-3
#1	Washington State	Home	Win	27-3
#1	Wisconsin	Away	Win	24-0
#1	Indiana	Away	Win	37-7
#1	Northwestern	Home	Win	60-0
#1	Illinois	Away	Win	30-0
#1	Michigan State	Home	Win	35-0
#1	Iowa	Home	Win	55-13
#1	Michigan (#4)	Away	Tie	10-10
#4	Southern Cal (#7)	Rose Bowl	Win	42-21

Final rank: 2nd AP; 3rd UPI

1974 (10-2)

Rank	Opponent (rank)	Site	Result	Score
#4	Minnesota	Away	Win	34-19
#2	Oregon State	Home	Win	51-10
#1	SMU	Home	Win	28-9
#1	Washington State	Away	Win	42-7
#1	Wisconsin (#13)	Home	Win	52-7
#1	Indiana	Home	Win	49-9
#1	Northwestern	Away	Win	55-7
#1	Illinois	Home	Win	49-7
#1	Michigan State	Away	Loss	13-16
#4	Iowa	Away	Win	35-10
#4	Michigan (#3)	Home	Win	12-10
#3	Southern Cal (#5)	Rose Bowl	Loss	17-18

Final rank: 4th AP; 3rd UPI

1975 (11-1)

Rank	Opponent (rank)	Site	Result	Score
#3	Michigan State (#11)	Away	Win	21-0
#3	Penn State (#7)	Home	Win	17-9
#2	North Carolina	Home	Win	32-7
#2	UCLA (#13)	Away	Win	41-20
#1	Iowa	Home	Win	49-0
#1	Wisconsin	Home	Win	56-0
#1	Purdue	Away	Win	35-6
#1	Indiana	Home	Win	24-14
#1	Illinois	Away	Win	40-3
#1	Minnesota	Home	Win	38-6
#1	Michigan (#4)	Home	Win	21-14
#1	UCLA (#11)	Rose Bowl	Loss	10-23

Final rank: 4th AP; 4th UPI

1976 (9-2-1)

Rank	Opponent (rank)	Site	Result	Score
#4	Michigan State	Home	Win	49-21
#2	Penn State (#7)	Away	Win	12-7
#2	Missouri	Home	Loss	21-22
#8	UCLA (#4)	Home	Tie	10-10
#10	Iowa	Away	Win	34-14
#9	Wisconsin	Away	Win	30-20
#9	Purdue	Home	Win	24-3
#8	Indiana	Away	Win	47-7
#8	Illinois	Home	Win	42-10
#8	Minnesota	Away	Win	9-3
#8	Michigan (#4)	Home	Loss	0-22
#11	Colorado (#12)	Orange Bowl	Win	27-10

Final rank: 5th AP; 5th UPI

1977 (9-3)

Rank	Opponent (rank)	Site	Result	Score
#5	Miami (Fla.)	Home	Win	10-0
#6	Minnesota	Home	Win	38-7
#4	Oklahoma (#3)	Home	Loss	28-29
#6	SMU	Away	Win	35-7
#4	Purdue	Home	Win	46-0
#5	Iowa	Away	Win	27-6
#4	Northwestern	Home	Win	35-15
#3	Wisconsin	Home	Win	42-0
#4	Illinois	Away	Win	35-0
#4	Indiana	Home	Win	35-7
#4	Michigan (#5)	Away	Loss	6-14
#9	Alabama (#3)	Sugar Bowl	Loss	6-35

Final rank: 11th AP; 12th UPI

1978 (7-4-1)

Rank	Opponent (rank)	Site	Result	Score
#6	Penn State (#5)	Home	Loss	0-19
#16	Minnesota	Away	Win	27-10
#13	Baylor	Home	Win	34-28
#14	SMU	Home	Tie	35-35
#16	Purdue	Away	Loss	16-27
NR	Iowa	Home	Win	31-7
NR	Northwestern	Home	Win	63-20
NR	Wisconsin	Away	Win	49-14
NR	Illinois	Home	Win	45-7
#19	Indiana	Away	Win	21-18
#16	Michigan (#6)	Home	Loss	3-14
#20	Clemson (#6)	Gator Bowl	Loss	15-17

Final rank: NR